the milk thief

For Joseph, Jack and Ioan.

PAUL HENRY

the milk thief

seren

seren
is the book imprint of
Poetry Wales Press Ltd
Wyndham Street, Bridgend, Wales

ISBN 1-85411-240-6

A CIP record for this title is available from
the British Library

*The publisher works with the financial assistance of the
Arts Council of Wales*

Cover: 'Thief' painting by Anthony Goble

Printed in Palatino by CPD Wales, Ebbw Vale

Contents

III. Newport East

I

Aber

Winnie's

I slide an arm into the cool
between sofa and cushion

                    (the pool
where the razor-shell waits)

                        find
what naturally swims to hand —

the sprung spectacle case she forgot
and

        priceless when opened out
to the sun
                his dappled frames

with her lenses inside them.

The Last Throws of Summer

*"Many throwers positively resent the intrusion
of a scientific explanation, preferring to keep
the magic unsullied...."*
Dr. Robert Reid (author:"The Physics of Boomerangs")

Open-mouthed, my sister's children
cram the small bay window
at the top of the Y.H.A. — on the beach
the British Boomerang Champion
from the floor below
is justifying the autographs
such notoriety demands.

All day he's gone out
(and, true to form, come back)
to move his car a fraction,
never quite content with its place.

In the dusk his crooked wand

                                                     vanishes

then reappears in his hand.

What choreographs his absurd dance
carves the boomerang tide's
endlessly perfected curve,
surfs the subtle air waves
between craft and technique.
His wife screams down to him at nine
and dutifully he returns.

Tomorrow he'll lay his loves
in sheaths, on a childless back seat,
reverse a final one hundred degrees
and leave, less icon than nagged librarian.

And my sister's eldest will gaze
at already fading parchments,
his lightweight signatures in the sand.

Lines Written Outside a *"Replica of a Sunshine Home For Blind Babies"*, Aberystwyth

Did no one take a brick to this glass case?
    A ball and chain?
Now I'm old enough to press my face
    to the brittle pane

without their ghostly hugs around my gaze
    it comes home —
how time's a shell of the snail it was,
    a smaller room.

What miniature, sunken eyes remain look out
    from a pantheon
that keeps this town's unstable light,
    as I look in,

trying to read the Braille of the years between,
    with no clear sign
but, conjured back and fore by the sun,
    their faces in mine.

Welsh Incident

In the early hours of September 3rd, 1997, a giant turtle was found dead, on the shoreline at Cricieth.

The Cambrian News reporter's car
blocks the lane down to the shore.

Someone plays the bagpipes
where the last field meets the sea.

But for the randomness of the tide
she'd still be gracing the waters
of a century as it drowned.

Armour-plated, run aground,
a creaturely grief mourns her end.

Two elderly, village paparazzi
circle the wreckage, take snaps
before the oceanographers descend.

The Hourglass

Ghosts of the architects move in.
Down town the moon floats
across Great Darkgate Street.

The hour gained finds my father
teasing the wheel through his hands
as if he'd invented time,

as if we could rise in his Bubble
up to the stars' infinite tides
and drift back home.

He breaks south of the pier
that creaks and leans out too far
on its zimmer-frame, points

to the same joke. *"By God!
It's Auntie Dwyn!"* (Victory
on her column) *"Still there."*

Cue my sister's Petula Clark,
her tiny womb's pod
already bursting into song.

*

The singer swallows eggs raw
and talks all day in whispers
before a recital, draws

a pebble-headed crowd.
It's her house of sighs,
her love that skews

like a gull between clouds,
that harbours lullabies.
When I clap she always bows.

13

*

The King's Hall and the Waun chapel
are still singing.

Sing in their heads.

Bethesda and Tabernacle.

Sing in their heads.
Sing in their heads.

Seilo and the castle choir.
Sing. Sing. Sing.

Tros y Garreg
Mynwent Eglwys

Dafydd y Garreg...
Ar Hyd y Nos

Sing. Sing.

Y Deryn Pur
Y Gwcw Fach

Y Ferch o'r Scer
Gwŷr Harlech...

Sing in their heads,
their grey, spectacled heads.

*

The sixties undress.
Flowers lay crumpled and strewn
in heaps along the coast.

My father looks down
from the salty rail,
his bald patch turning brown.

14

*

Wil T. and I

squint through slats
on hands and knees,
avoid the sperm whale spits

of the rising tide.
The gipsy's wink,
once mechanized,

dooms us to *DRINK
TOO MUCH AND DIE.*
(Her luminous tank

dispenses cards
that smell of ash).
We can't afford

a second wish.
Between the boards
our futures flash.

Just before they hit
the rocks they fly.

*

The giant paper bellows
sigh, page after page,
shaken back to shape like pillows.

I put it down to age.

*

Ann Walters, town soprano,
waving her daughter off
down intricate lines

15

remembers to give
one last tip, her shout
more of a recitative

as the train pulls out.
"Julia!
Don't forget!

Packet sooooooooooooup!"

Slowly, bar by bar,
her back to the engine,
my sister forgives her.

*

They chime through the dark
like perfectly struck tuning forks,

walk out without keys
under the unswept stars.

Old needles clatter onto the lawn.
His treeful of *I.O.U.'s* holds on.

The moon diminished, at daylight
the first notes take flight.

The piano between them has aired
the spirit of unloved wood.

She waits nervously in her gown.
Nobody counts her in.

She opens her mouth to sing
and the silence is deafening.

*

Sprawled out on murderous carpets
    I play with the same toys —
the unicycling clown, the snow-dome,
    the bear with insomniac eyes...

or pick up *Gulliver's Travels*
    by its page eared at 51,
oblivious to all but the music
    until the quiet draws in

and I drift about in search of them —
    the voice and the violin —
wander into dust-showered rooms
    as if after something stolen,

panic to find in the furniture
    their misplaced harmonies.
Tears scale down the stairs.
    I watch the waterline rise...

    wake up tethered
where stone looks shine
on the bay's draining board

    and washed up lines
I'd fish for at first light
are weighted, snagged, entwined

    about the rocks' lie,
where the hour's glass, caught
    in pools, momentarily,

    sees them walk, side
by side, my sighing family,
    into the oncoming tide.

Calcutta Sandals

Thirty years after the war and still
your sluggish toes would emerge
for summer, indecently.

                    The struggle
to slip the small, braided noose
over the big one embarrassed me.

Flesh and chappal curled at the edges.

And yet they smelt fatherly,
like your Bombay watchstrap,
gave credence to your sermons.

After shoreline forays,
you'd slap their soles together
like a self-applauding seal

then put them out
to dry on the back step.

Until the warm air finally cooled
on those long, August evenings
and, like all the other clutter

with which a minister's son,
who washed his feet in blood,
chose to brand so many

(the tiny elephants, unpacked
half their original size,

your tin trunk's moth-eaten dhoti,

the untouchable hookah...)

they came apart in your hands.

Six Houses

for Ann Walters Henry

Your songs filled six houses,
each one to the brim.
Big arias wandered from kitchen to hall,
from landing to living room.

Silence curled up in drawers
and knew its time would come,
like the rest of us, to be moved.
I thought that every home

similarly sang.
On hearing *Qui la voce...*
the hound melted into the rug.
(You claimed he had perfect pitch).

Aspiring divas visited
your *Queen Of The Night*; slaves
to no one, they ate your scones
then left for exotic lives.

You chose instead to raise the rooves
of the houses in our hearts,
marking every restless move
by pulling the piano apart

before the *Pickfords* men arrived.
Six houses, one mansion now
that outlives us all.
I crouch outside its windows,

cup an ear, hear resonate
your deepest, most haunting note.

Waunfawr

My mother's coffee morning crew,
their wrinkled smiles turned cold,
their haloes rinsed blue,

are not so much old
as suddenly wrecked by love
in a strange town. Only the gold

on the rim of an ear's cove,
a cup's tilted ring
or a mast-like crucifix was saved.

I remember the bright billowing
of their sails on the balcony,
that caught the wind blowing

twenty years too late. Now the sea
sips away at her tired crew
and empty china stares back at me.

Something Beginning With...

Too tired to spy the last clue
the camper by my side
sinks another summer deeper
into motherhood and sighs.
Something beginning with love
finds me inside a sheath
that hugs my past like ice
around a Paleolithic tooth.

I am Anon who begat Anon
who begat Simply Because
and all the loves and murderers
whose kisses and blood
haunt this groundsheet's DNA.
Press your ear to the earth
and almost hear my heart.
Mourn this strata of family graves.

The stars turn to ash
emptied over us as rain.
A rumour that started out at sea
grows louder with each groan.
Soon there'll be lightning,
the reins of the tent in the wind's
ancient hands, the canvas galloping on,
she'll wake and ask for the letter again.

Holiday Home

This house, built on clay, the last
to slide into the sea,
splits its sides with parting cracks
by those who signed the book:

the Burns of Slough, 1959 —
"This Shangri-La of Wales must never die!"...

Dunkirk's very own
Dot & Ken, June '65 —
"Flymo broken. Shears first class!"...

and, lest we forget, *"Rex The P-o-ET!"*
whose pawprint authenticates
some doggerel from 1972.

The Burns return in '86, retired,
smug, children's professions listed
as if it counted — Accountant, G.P.,
Lawyer and... one missing
from *"Our Infamous Four!"*

Thirty-nine summers

assembled and folded away
neatly, into a fractured box,
like jigsaws, cards or dominoes

lined up purely to be felled
by the tide, which raises the stakes
with each turned over wave.

Here's the owner, Spring '98:
Hilary B — *"Down for repairs,
to keep this place afloat!"*

I take in her skewed watercolours
and books, half-comforted
that someone still flies with Biggles,
pedals, bare-kneed, to Smuggler's Top
up the stairwell's 1 in 1.

Happy to sleep, to squat
almost imperially
on these suspect foundations,

I turn in the same, creaking lie
as those who signed its sheets
eloquently, with love,

whose breakages, like mine,
are paid for by the sea's refrain —

Come back... come back... come back...

Z Loves A

after R.S. Thomas

We went to the same school,
shared the same back seat haze
that ushered us on between lanes,
became fluent in David Bowie,
the innuendoes of songs —
Changes, Wild Is The Wind,
Life on Mars....

Supposing I finally call,
bony beagle in tow,
stammer my name to the microphone
lodged in your fine, calligraphic gate.
Supposing your voice crackles back
like an old '78
and the gate opens,
and the roses that line your drive
explode into stars,
and the gravel underfoot grinds
twenty years to dust,
and the man who sold the world
is ushered in
by the woman who bought it back

to waltz across chequered tiles
in a stately hall

or simply to share the smoke rings
dancing in two china cups

while out on the lawn
my ghostly hound
sniffs about your stardust

as if the scent had never died.

Burning Old Loves

I rest my hand on the spayed cat,
the scar where the knife left its mark,

take in the bookish peat, our love's
Night Of The Long Knives,

read the dead wood as it sparks.
Only the wrought iron implements

and a parched *Examiner* in the grate
survive us, your cryptic annotations

in my copy of *The Wasteland*
flowering still in the margins of thought.

And what else?... Heat? Prolific rain?
Our smiles in the palm of a friend?

The cat's tail strays under my chin.
Bowed lightly, she starts to purr again.

Aber

"Her different world was added to the world"
'The Birth of Venus at Aberystwyth' — *John Ormond*

Deaf to the shipping forecast —

Love.

Blind to red flags, grey mist —

Love.

The truth in history's
myth-riddled veins —

Love.

Chaplin in oilskins —

Love.

*

He rides the sly propeller's swarm
across no man's time.

    Victory
may be stoned but she worries
about him when he declines
the lifebelt she extends.

      He leans
out of the tide race of his past,
the diagonal of a line cast
decades ago

   and diminishing
from a rudder.

    He sings.

*

Try the smaller lenses now.
Look for *Aber* on the bow.

Bottled inside binoculars
the unread letters of wars,
famines and races
flap on feathered traces,
pour themselves out
at his sandalled feet.

He guts the mackerel,
hunched in the tiny hull,
with keel precision
slices open

the envelopes; this one...
this one... this one...

launches heads and tails
and then entrails
back into the dark
his white sail bookmarked

finds her letters, hidden
in the scaled tome of a sewen
that swam too far
from the mouth of the river:

Dear Nerites,

I think about you less each day.
The stars and the moon drift away.
The harbour's chimed jewellery
trickles back into the sea.
I think about you less each day....

Dear, dear Ares,

Life loves on, a sweet decay
of fruit stares out across the bay
and stares away your memory
and stares away your memory.
I think about you less each day....

My own Hephaestus,

The tide that turns all words to clay
shakes this glass. I hear you say
"By these lips remember me"
then taste the salt of history,
the tide that turns all words to clay....

Dearest Anchises,

I think about you less each day,
watch the white clouds sail away,
sail away your memory,
sail away your memory.
I think about you less each day....

P.S. I love you Eros,
Pygmalion, Adonis....

*

He's drowned cities away,
beyond Caerwyddno's buoy,

tuning into a frequency
no sooner found

than lost at sea....

*

No flowers, no doves
but frayed white handkerchiefs
decorate the driftwood
that was *Aber*,

       home on the tide.

      *

Should similar winds find you,
  coughing up dreams, alone
in some room, some dry city,
  less heart than bone,

let it be her ghost that seeps
  through the landlord's walls,
like sea through the closed lips
  of a dark, tenanted shell.

Let it be her wreck to haunt —
  your bed of regrets,
and her last kiss, in the end,
  come back to it

through suddenly sun-drenched nets.

Moving On

A nail's sundial fades on the bedroom wall.
Five hours ago I watched as families
like ours dismantled frail territories
on a cooling beach, left tiny flags
to the memory of the sea (our cries
on the fold of a blue infinity)

                           then raised
an abandoned bucket, realised
too late its castle's ruin, your smile
tuned to a shell, its vast aeolian womb.
You tuned it in turn to my ear, shared
the hush of infinite keys.

                       The tide came in.
Now sand lodges in every cove of our love,
(both of us roughly the same cracked mould),
hides between the silences, slides down
through summers, homes, our hourglass with legs.

II

The Visitors

The Visitors

The women of my earliest years
fill this room's empty bay
without warning —

Brown Helen,
Catrin Sands, Gwyneth Blue,
Nightingale Ann...

Their songs
return to a stranger's hand
the keys to all past tenancies,

Heulwen, Dwynwen, Bron Y Llan...

I lie back, let them haunt,
the soft pulse of their lips
against the stone wall I've become,

Heather, Geta, Prydwen Jane...

listen hard across the dark
as their voices fade again,

Edith Smart, St Julia...

sleep with the bedroom door ajar
in case they should drift back in.

Brown Helen

Floats on a cushion
in the parlour at *Penllain*.
The sun through frayed nets
drowns the smell of must.
A plankton of dust
swims in the space between us.

"I saw you. Don't look down.
You picked it,
then you rolled it
then you flicked it.
I saw you!"

Were she not so brown
and terrifyingly thin
and certain a witness

I might have surfaced sooner
without salt in my eyes.

Catrin Sands

"Ready about... lee-oh!"

Cabin-boy to her Bligh
I need to hook a bass
then cook it for her sandy hair.

Instead, it's sea sickness
I catch, and blue, blue air.

Gwyneth Blue

Locked in the lifeboat shed
with Nightingale Ann.

What if no one had come —
not the tide, nor the sun

nor love,
nor love's Harbour Master, birth?

And what if the gun
out on the horizon
had never sounded?

She emerges into the light,
shielding her laughter.

Following swiftly after
her petticoat's wake,

the handsome blue boat
slides out

on its way to save.

Nightingale Ann

She'd raise one brow
like the circumflex over the *o* in *môr*

or that curved bough
arching the Dwyfor,
her River Lachrymose.

I laid my poacher's lines at her feet
and traced a tear's course
from cheek to lip, then tasted it.

She told me the history of her rings,
the vocabulary of birdsong.

"Look away" she said
and, fool, I did,

turning back to a half-dressed tree
her blue eyes poured into,
a sudden shoal of leaves at my feet

and, on the stone where she sat,
a small circle of salt.

Heulwen

Still holding on to the sea rail
I taste and imagine another life
that's slippery with the salt of her bones.

"Too much whiskylight.

Get back to that dark house,
its tea and antiquity,
its po and shotgun under the bed,

its attic clouds

conveying the summer's regattas elsewhere."

So I lie one more night
by the old oak screen
with candles and eyebright,

lie one more night
in the flowerlight
with heather and celandine,

lie one more night
by the old oak screen

with sand in my hair
and salt in my dreams —
craving another *dead dear.*

Dwynwen

Her necklace snaps
in the Coliseum, spills
its countless ways.

        A crab
between the shushing aisles
I glance up to the light
and see

       Dwynwen's bride,
deaf as a silent movie,
hurling flowers at small girls.

I can't find her pearls,
am drowning in feet

and now she wants to join me
down here —

       the loudest whisper
in the universe, her accent
perfectly preserved

belonging to the child
who, to *The End*,

must live out her dreams underwater.

Bron Y Llan

Of the sharp words and the blackberry tarts
and the poultice that drew out the black thorn
from this hand

      which warms her wagging scorn
in a fountain pen,

      her suddenly bleeding heart.

Heather

Forgive me this apple I stole
some thirty years ago

when your hair was brown, and mine
as fair as this four-year-old's

who offers it back to you now
sweet Heather, hauntingly.

Is it summer or autumn?
The years collect on the lawn.

You show us the latest extension
to the house time almost didn't see.

Then you start to cry as, guiltily,
I lift my shadow up to your tree.

Geta

She's a fine white yacht
a cool airy distance away.

Make space for her, make space.

Make space and you will notice
she's drifting nearer the shore.

Make space, make space.

You have waited long enough
for this love to harbour.

Prydwen Jane

Even more mystified once
right now she'd settle for mad,
at eighty outliving me to shame —
Africa, Egypt, the Philippines...
but she wants more *"time, time, time..."*
and shakes her fist at God
along the quiet lane to Cei Bach.

She repeats the latest: Prydwen, in transit,
from Florida to Gatwick,
the only nurse on a doctorless plane,
instructing the pilot whether to land
in Atlanta or go *"on, on, on..."*
at the casual flick of her hand.
Though here, in the quiet lane to Cei Bach,

she shudders inside my donkey-jacket,
fragile, angry still
from the sight of Gwyneth Blue's grave,
as we pass by the unbleating loves,
glimpse the bay's shimmering lull,
"witness, witness, witness..." the sunset
ending the quiet lane to Cei Bach.

Edith Smart

Diving into her blue dress
she leaves another creaking board,
admits the awkward fit of her age
then rises to break the surface

of another day, *Edith Beatrice
Walters* — swimmer, talker, pianist,
playing a till's dissonant keys,
cleaving the ham, turning its page

across a counter's glass bay,
abusing the gift, seizing the joints,
drowning home at six to play
Mendelssohn's *Songs Without Words*.

St Julia

Dancing to Motown in her room
with Brown Helen and Catrin Sands.
She might be teaching me how to swim —
first the breast-stroke, with hands
that open and drift like seaweed
into reverse, now the suntanned
front crawl.... Their skirts wind
like mermaids' tails in the gloom.
The scales fall away.

There's barely time
to realign white headbands
between tracks, to suddenly become
The Supremes, to apportion blame
for wrong steps, to further dim
the lights,

to mime a scream.

III

Newport East

Newport East

The booths close in two hours.
Ice-cream vans are on overtime.
Twinkle, twinkle... Arthur Scargill's
voice passes down the hill.
"...The only TRUE Socialist candidate..."
is addressing the slow sunset,
fathoms deeper by the word.
The Town's coral gathers about them —
the sun and Arthur Scargill,
going down together,
one gracefully, one burning still.

Sacred Ground

Her one, wire-haired wing
sweeps the path away
like a habit of waves...
swish... eroding a wall.

A resinous air in the leaves
has bowed its way home.

At the silver ladder's foot,
on a zed-bed's full span,
Jacob, her son, between Art
and C.D.T., dreams
a catwalk of angels.

Dressed in chamois-leathers
they scale up and down the rungs,
are building a nest under the eaves
beside an unhatched burglar alarm.

The muffled chimes of unshod soles
flit soothingly across a shed
she has christened *The Church*.

Rare moments when the tide abates
she disappears into its arch
where sunlight stains the knots
and fires arrows through the slats.

A gull on an aerial's crucifix
ruffles the plot
of her small allotment of sky

as Jacob's transistor wakes
to drown with Heavy Metal
the tolling of angelic feet,

his mother's one-winged whisperings
along the worn down path.

The Glebelands

Boats, like fallen window-boxes
sink in mud, bloom with weeds.

Bulbous-headed kids on the bank
manoeuvre first bikes like drunks.

One turn of a trussed back-wheel,
a puddled rut's watermill

and see them, performing tricks
in streets named after Romantics.

(Alf sniffs at a chained gate
where Sam inhales Bill's shit).

The old art school's rusted dome
hangs in a Turneresque haze.

All seasons are skewed enough
and the river pedals after the sun.

Footballers surface, draped in gold
like tired, hungover gods,

know these are green as any fields
for faintly heroic dreams.

Monopod washing lines spin
their anemometers of love.

Churchbells rattle their crates.
The paint flakes off the trees.

Hook and Needle

He'd rest his rod in the V
while she stayed in the Robin,
knitting something white or pink,
emerging only to empty the flask

or to be led, discreetly,
down an aisle of leaves
at the side of the bridge
then under the biggest arch.

Click-click went the reel, all evening.
Click-click from daylight to dark
as the line stirred, then pulled
then slackened and came back in.

And later still, barely visible,
on opposite sides of the glass,
they'd mime catches that swung,
hers from a needle, his from a hook

before the full spool of their love
unwound on its three wheels —
click-click, over the narrow bridge,
click-click, to somewhere less picturesque,

threading a thin trail of smoke
through the leafy eye of the dusk.

The Milk Thief

When sleep takes over the watch
I dream of him, darkly dressed,
stealing up the stone steps
somewhere between four and five,
leaving no prints,
only damp, luckless horseshoes.

He puts his lips
to the last drops of motherhood.

A leaking tap's blown glass
pulls and slips, rhythmically,
inside the night's stagnancy.

The Milk Thief outwits me again.

Drifting down to the kitchen
catches the first hooves of rain.

Inside The *MIND* Shop

The fake snow-spray's giant kiss
in the mirror's *Merry Xmas*
marks the spot that wills to fit
the giant into the midget.

A finger skates on the counter's pane
where a baby's boot waits to be claimed,
where Ritchie, phone tucked under his chin,
might be playing the violin
or conducting *Silent Night*,

where records, shoes, books and ties
are memorials to the Seventies,
where there's time to contemplate
the third world stuff — rugs, cushions,
a carved bird, skull caps....

A club-foot kicks a box of cups.
Mary glances out from her wig,
hugs her faded *Woman's Own*
with its haloed baby on the front.
Something of everyone is wanted.

The dead on rails drip at the cuffs
with tags, beyond bar-codes
absorb the rain brought in,
a charmed sprig of incense.

A mitten picks up a snow dome
and shakes another storm
for the figurine children on their farm
who've seen it all before.

The door's cowbell does not distract
the one surviving browser.
He stares himself out in the mirror,
clears his throat and, suitcase in tow,
tries another *Ho! Ho! Ho!*

Pissing On Graves

Wayne Isaac I wrestled you to the floor
of these boys' toilets at Noman's High.
Its tiles shone with rain and urine,
our daily inscribed epitaph
still fresh on its glazed stone —
So dribbled his life away.

Your blazer stank of cigarettes,
your breath of whisky.
Your tongue could cut to shreds,
sharpened itself on our blunt heads.
The years slid and rolled us on
into the same hissing trough.

Yours then, this wasted brilliance,
this sunlit arc of piss.
Your carefully inked initials outlive
those who chanted for blood,
whose steps soon dripped away
with caretakers' campanology.

Freedom fighters of your class
never made the plaque in the hall.
Old Blackcap's sonorous roll call
hardly paused for those who slipped off
angrily, into the dark chasms
between the names on the wall.

So let this marble remember you,
your brief, private war,
at the going down of another day
and the weakening of my last
limpid signature
which trickles down a black hole.

I glance up to the skylight.
A cloud's rendering cracks

and the first star in the universe
makes its mark.

                  Heavy feet
pass beyond frosted glass,

leak along infinite corridors.

Builders

The roll of a kanga drill through the wall
and Buddy's pushing back the years,
digging that gravel's applause.

He pauses, centre-stage, half-way
between the roses and the skip,
kisses the comb's mike at his lips.

Three schoolgirls stare up
chewing gum, as another trowel
scrapes across the sky.

He takes a bow,
picks up his barrow
then tips another load away

a-hey, a-hey-hey....

The Park Girls

Belch like toads at closing time
and pitch their laughter in keys
sopranos dream about.

The wind pushes their empty swings,
the rusty cogs and pendulums
of a clock beyond repair.

Round and round the park they go,
disturbing the inertia of a town
that turns, anti-clockwise,

about their screams.
Small crimes confess themselves
between the barbed railings —

a hairgrip pinches a condom's
stocking top, a needle
lurks in the buttercups.

In the searchlights of a car
they balance on heels, arms out
like novice tight-rope walkers.

Even the rain can't tame them.
They shelter inside the arms
of a tree and start to sing.

Through Green Railings

Prints in the long-jump sand,
a woman's feet and hands.

The space between take off and land,
what was it? The difference between

the earth and the moon,
the first kiss and the honeymoon?

All those years in flight.
I cling to the railings' measured light

and think I catch her shadow flit
in a gull's.

          For a second's breeze
the missed trajectories

of her love and mine synchronize,
hold hands in mid air,

turn to smile at each other
on the leap's highest tower

and kiss...

          before the ecstatic climb

lets go

          falls back down out of time.

Fifty-fifty

Hers

the wire necklace
that chokes the young man's cenotaph,
that suspects flowers.

His

the defeated castle
stumbling into a river of lies.

Hers

the midnight freight
rolling her heart away.

His

the furnace flames
stubbed out
on the stars' ashtray.

Hers

the smile that cools
then hardens on steel frames.

His

the moon.

Hers

its handkerchiefs.

His

the wind only roofers bless,
that fleeces a church roof
as slates loosen like vows.

Hers

this pavement's leaf,
swept on by a sudden breeze
towards a new life....

Hey Diddle-diddle

Here's only the eloquence of sleep
finding its tongue, the last sheep
hurdling the cemetery stone,
the bleat of abandoned head-phones,

only the knives and forks talking,
the dogs and spoons barking.
A soft-shoe-shuffle disappears
into smooth, arched ears.

Falsetto boughs break.
The tom in the moon aches
to hear their lullabies, makes a wish.
The years turn cold in his dish.

The wind bows a pylon's *A*.
Small dreams are still at play.
Starved quadrupeds on the plain
ignore the passing train.

Ghosts

A leather belt snakes off a chair.
The cellophane slough of a French loaf
squirms on a wicker tray.
A tiger smoulders by candlelight.

I'd have you drift upstream our love,
leave three babies on its banks
and head to where the dream began,
turn and trace along its thread
with a rusty hook in your soft lips.
And then lay on your stretch of silk
any remnant we might have missed
or lost or shed — the stone
that fitted your hand like a promise,
a sawn trunk's fresh rings,
a congregation of flies, or bats,
or hoarse sheep, or the bull
that wouldn't budge his eyes,
or an eel that flashed in a pool.

I'd have you enquire of our ghosts
if they haunt us happily

and if they saw this flickering room
in the dusk of that first kiss.

*

Earlier, in your tartan pyjamas,
you said you'd forgo the fire
and join me underground, but that first
you needed to change your hair.

Now under these leaves,
deep in your tartan pyjamas,
you lie more warmly than I
and I daren't touch the earth as it breathes
for loving it too much

but listen instead to the breeze
rattling old and brittle frames.

Acknowledgements

Some of these poems first appeared in the following publications: *Beyond Bedlam* (Anvil), *Christmas in Wales* (Seren), *Interchange, London Magazine, The New Welsh Review, Oxford Poetry, Planet, Poetry Wales, Poetry Review, Thumbscrew, The Times Literary Supplement, The Western Mail.*

The Poem 'Sacred Ground' was one of five responses to the theme of 'Angels', commissioned by the 1998 Hay Festival's Poetry Squantum event.

I am grateful to the Arts Council of Wales, for the *Published Writer's Bursary* which helped in the completion of this book.